Many do important jobs or have secret stories to tell. You can find out about some of my favorite bugs and their fantastic beetle relatives in this book. M.P.

Look
for one special beetle that's hiding in every picture. You can find out more about it on the last page.

Beetles and bugs come in all shapes
and sizes. They have been around for millions
of years and there are many different kinds.
Some are beautiful, but watch out—
not all of them look so friendly...